SMART ABOUT SPORTS

Meet the Dodgers

By
Mike Kennedy

with **Mark Stewart**

NORWOOD HOUSE PRESS

Norwood House Press, P.O. Box 316598, Chicago, Illinois 60631

For information regarding Norwood House Press,
please visit our website at: www.norwoodhousepress.com or call 866-565-2900.

Photo Credits:
    Getty Images (4, 16), Associated Press (7, 15, 22), Icon SMI (8, 20), SportsChrome (12, 13, 21, 23 both),
    Black Book Partners (18).
Cover Photos:
    Top Left: Topps, Inc.; Top Right: Lisa Blumenfeld/Getty Images; Bottom Left: Jeff Gross/Getty Images;
    Bottom Right: Topps, Inc.
The baseball memorabilia photographed for this book is part of the authors' collection:
    Page 6) Don Drysdale Card: Mitock & Sons; Page 10) Zack Wheat Card: Recruit Little Cigars; Duke Snider Magazine: Select
    Publications, Inc.; Roy Campanella Card: Topps, Inc.; Dazzy Vance Button: Cracker Jack/F.W. Ruckheim & Brother;
    Page 11) Sandy Koufax Card, Steve Garvey Card, Orel Hershiser Card, Fernando Valenzuela Card: Topps, Inc.

Special thanks to Topps, Inc.

Editor: Brian Fitzgerald
Designer: Ron Jaffe
Project Management: Black Book Partners, LLC.
Editorial Production: Jessica McCulloch

LIBRARY OF CONGRESS CATALOGING-IN-PUBLICATION DATA
    Kennedy, Mike (Mike William), 1965-
    Meet the Dodgers / by Mike Kennedy with Mark Stewart.
        p. cm. -- (Smart about sports)
    Includes bibliographical references and index.
    Summary: "An introductory look at the Los Angeles Dodgers baseball team.
Includes a brief history, facts, photos, records, glossary, and fun
activities"--Provided by publisher.
    ISBN-13: 978-1-59953-371-1 (library edition : alk. paper)
    ISBN-10: 1-59953-371-5 (library edition : alk. paper)
    1. Los Angeles Dodgers (Baseball team)--Juvenile literature. I. Stewart,
Mark, 1960- II. Title.
    GV875.L6K46 2010
    796.357'640979494--dc22

                                2009043047

Manufactured in the United States of America in North Mankato, Minnesota.
179R—042011

Contents

Words in **bold type** are defined on page 24.

The Dodgers play hard and love to win.

The Los Angeles Dodgers

Any baseball team would be proud to say, "We changed the game." The Dodgers really did. Long ago, the big leagues did not welcome players with dark skin. In 1947, the Dodgers thought it was time for a change. They put an African-American star named Jackie Robinson on the team. Baseball was never the same again!

Once Upon a Time

The Dodgers started in Brooklyn, New York. In 1958, they moved across the country to Los Angeles, California. The Dodgers have always put great players on the field. Don Drysdale and Jackie Robinson are just two of them.

Jackie Robinson was the first African-American player in the big leagues.

At Dodger Stadium, fans can watch a game and see the mountains.

At the Ballpark

The Dodgers play their home games in Dodger Stadium. It opened in 1962. It is one of the most beautiful ballparks in baseball. There are more seats here than in any other baseball stadium. From many of those seats, fans get pretty views of the California mountains.

Shoe Box

The cards, pins, and magazines on these pages belong to the authors. They show some of the best Dodgers ever.

Zack Wheat

Outfielder • 1909–1926
Zack Wheat was a great hitter. The ball seemed to jump off his bat. He played in more games than any other Dodger.

Duke Snider

Outfielder • 1947–1962
Duke Snider had a strong arm and a powerful swing. He hit more than 300 home runs during the 1950s.

Roy Campanella

Catcher • 1948–1957
Roy Campanella was the NL Most Valuable Player (MVP) three times. "Campy" was the first catcher to hit 40 home runs in a season.

Dazzy Vance

Pitcher

•1922–1932 & 1935
Dazzy Vance had a great fastball. He led the National League (NL) in strikeouts seven years in a row.

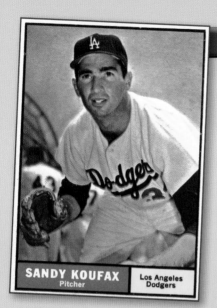

Sandy Koufax

Pitcher • 1955–1966
Sandy Koufax had a big bending curveball and a sizzling fastball. He pitched four no-hitters during his career.

SANDY KOUFAX
Pitcher

Los Angeles
Dodgers

Steve Garvey

First Baseman • 1969–1982
Steve Garvey was a good hitter and a great fielder. He helped the Dodgers reach the World Series four times.

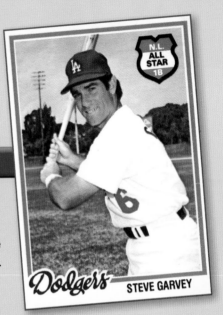

Dodgers STEVE GARVEY

Fernando Valenzuela

Pitcher • 1980–1990
Fernando Valenzuela was only 19 when he joined the Dodgers. He was baseball's biggest star in the early 1980s.

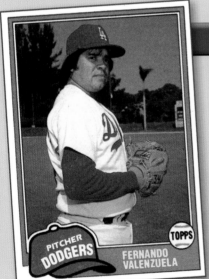

PITCHER
DODGERS
FERNANDO VALENZUELA
TOPPS

Orel Hershiser

Pitcher

• 1983–1994 & 2000
Orel Hershiser was nicknamed the "Bulldog." He once pitched 59 innings in a row without giving up a run.

DODGERS
OREL HERSHISER

ABC's of Baseball

In this picture of Andre Ethier, how many things can you find that begin with the letter **D**?

See page 23 for answer.

13

Brain Games

Here is a poem about a famous Dodger:

There once was a shortstop named Maury,
Who helped lead the Dodgers to glory.
When he stole second base,
It was not a fair race.
And that was the end of the story.

Guess which one of these facts is **TRUE**:

- *Maury Wills was the first player to steal 100 bases in a season.*

- *Maury was a great power hitter.*

See page 23 for answer.

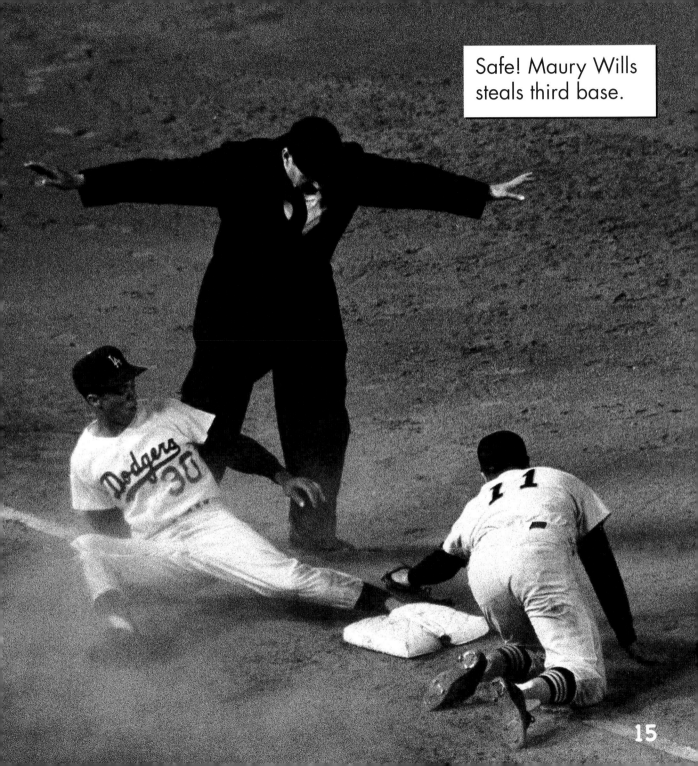

Safe! Maury Wills steals third base.

Casey Blake autographs a ball for a fan.

16

Fun on the Field

Fans have a great time when they go to Dodger Stadium. Before games, the players often take time to sign autographs. During games, the fans sing and dance to music between innings. They bat around beach balls. They also love to eat tasty hot dogs known as Dodger Dogs.

On the Map

The Dodgers call Los Angeles, California home. The players come from all over the country—and all over the world. Match these **Cy Young Award** winners with the places where they were born:

1 **Don Newcombe** • 1956 Cy Young Award
Madison, New Jersey

2 **Mike Marshall** • 1974 Cy Young Award
Adrian, Michigan

3 **Fernando Valenzuela** • 1981 Cy Young Award
Navojoa, Sonora, Mexico

4 **Orel Hershiser** • 1988 Cy Young Award
Buffalo, New York

5 **Eric Gagne** • 2003 Cy Young Award
Montreal, Quebec, Canada

United States Map

The Dodgers play
in Los Angeles, California.

World Map

What's in the Locker?

Baseball teams wear different uniforms for home games and away games. The Los Angeles home uniform is bright white. The uniform top spells out **D-O-D-G-E-R-S** in blue script lettering.

Russell Martin wears the team's home uniform.

The Los Angeles away uniform is gray. The uniform top spells out **L-O-S A-N-G-E-L-E-S**. The players wear a blue cap with the letters **L-A** on the front.

James Loney wears the team's away jersey.

We Won!

The Dodgers won their first World Series in 1955. They won their sixth in 1988.

That year, the team's star slugger, Kirk Gibson, was badly hurt before the World Series started. But he was still able to swing the bat. In the ninth inning of Game 1, Gibson hit a home run to win the game. The Dodgers won the next three games to win the World Series.

Kirk Gibson celebrates his famous home run.

Record Book

These Dodgers stars set amazing team records.

Hitter	Record	Year
Babe Herman	.393 **Batting Average**	1930
Tommy Davis	153 **Runs Batted In**	1962
Shawn Green	49 Home Runs	2001

Pitcher	Record	Year
Bob Caruthers	40 Wins	1889
Sandy Koufax	382 Strikeouts	1965
Eric Gagne	55 **Saves**	2003

Answer for ABC's of Baseball

Here are words in the picture that start with **D**:
Dirt, Dodger, Dugout.
Did you find any others?

Answer for Brain Games

The first fact is true. Maury Wills stole 104 bases
in 1962. In 16 seasons with the Dodgers, he hit only
17 home runs.

Baseball Words

BATTING AVERAGE
A measure of how often a batter gets a hit. A .300 average is very good.

CY YOUNG AWARD
The award given to the best pitcher in each league at the end of each season.

RUNS BATTED IN
The number of runners that score on a batter's hits and walks.

SAVES
A number that shows how many times a pitcher comes into a game and completes a win for his team.

Index

Photos are on **bold** numbered pages.

About the Dodgers

Learn more about the Dodgers at losangeles.dodgers.mlb.com

Learn more about baseball at www.baseballhalloffame.org